DANCES
LEFT
TO
LOVE

∞ ∞ ∞

JAMIE SHAW

Paperback: 978-1-964035-00-0
eBook: 978-1-964035-01-7
Library of Congress Control Number: 2024905731

This is a work of nonfiction.

SWEETSPIRE LITERATURE
——— MANAGEMENT ———

for Mother

This Is Not a Poem

[one]

This is not a poem, this is not a song.
This is just a charlatan, stringing you along.

Collecting thoughts can weigh you down,
For love that daren't come
Is nectar's port in clay or clown,
As, haw for ev'ry hum,

I'm pondering an almost friend,
The one, for whom do mount
My teardrops—hoping to contend
That *almost doesn't count.*

Thus, in a springtime lingering,
Our cherry blossoms young,
I ache to think I'm tinkering
Adieus upon her tongue.

Christmas isn't too far hence,
When carols I shall merge
With all the others—recompence
For Babel's tribal dirge.

Dances Left to Love

[two]

His poetry's poetic, fann'd
By heart within his song:
His bond is energetic, pann'd
To glisten and belong.

Perhaps he is a gard'ner—now
He's tending to his buds;
Or possibly a farmer, now
Unearthing dinner spuds.

There is a lass who buries psalms
Delicious wishes claim—
As, dying in adoring arms,
That kiss without a name,

Each night, beneath a photograph,
His candle stick she lights,
To put to bed the other half
Of love his leaving writes.

Take her down to rivers gone,
To dances left to love,
And he will find her ever wan—
In passion's eager grove.

JAMIE SHAW

Smudges

three

Father, hear these words I pray,
The way I want to be:
The way I wasn't yesterday—
In love, on bended knee.

Before I buy, I seize the day,
Aware of its deceit:
Let sunshine be my popinjay,
And caution my conceit.

Somewhere someone's a friend of mine—
At least, that hope remains;
Be thou my vision, I'll be thine,
Till broken lie my chains.

I dreamt of her the night before,
When union came and went—
To contravene what you adore,
In passion prized and lent.

My heart just isn't in it, Lord,
Like smudges on a page
From which a nous, astutely pour'd,
Deflects an honest rage.

Love Not Lost

[four]

This poem isn't wrought in sport,
In case it doesn't gel:
Your eyes can make its shrift as short
As swoops you render fell.

A word to make you clucky, fey,
An aphorism rare,
Are wheels for your lucky day,
Discovering a spare.

Why bother? If you're killing time,
You're playing with its fire—
Spirit swill, reborn to climb,
Audacious, in a pyre...

She is my little Angel Fish—
If I'm her King George Whiting,
A stinky tinker's her delicious
Wishing well, in writing.

So, if, evolving, love not lost
Evolves a womb for me,
I'm quick enough to pay the cost
Our bodies bode to be.

Sophia

Sophia's wise beyond her years,
In fact, I'm making up
Existence crowned with blood and tears—
For succour's latent cup

Is hope, so worth her love a while,
Heart's epitome,
To occupy her rank and file
With each bit of me.

But, strange to say, she doesn't pay
The price to so belong—
To hold up sunlight to the day,
And write it down in song.

Great is the woman, bright the girl,
And somewhere here I am—
To love of greater price the pearl
Is honey for her jam.

Philosophy? Believing now,
I read between the lines:
Sophia's mine to plant or plough—
As recreation pines.

For Eva

[six]

If *en avant* the one I want
Is climbing on a bus,
I'll write her in a diff'rent font,
To rhyme for both of us.

Such pure glues we choose to ooze—
That is, if I am hers
To read between the lines, peruse
The eloquence she purrs...

But not a word is our exchange,
A single line to swap—
I give up hope, to rearrange
Concession on the hop.

Her body is a work in which
Sweet spirit honours wings,
As beauty you propose to hitch
Meets universal things.

For now her tartan pantomime
Resides here in my heart—
An embryonic paradigm
For comeliness, and art.

No Rest for the Wicked

From broken limbs a broken soul
Lies bleeding in the gap:
'Twixt sunrise for the mare in foal—
And evolution's sap.

For He, so wicked, so they say,
Must invocate a word:
Forgive me if I go astray,
If silence be preferr'd...

In cubicles we huddle, wait
On Jesus, killing time,
Lest *hubris* wipe a muddy slate—
Is turpitude a crime?

Madman, can you read my mind?
The Cobra has his look
So diamond-hard, so unrefined—
A pall the World forsook.

If Hope be wicked, Love as bad,
And Charity insane,
They may be fads I never had—
In dreams I entertain.

Another List

[eight]

The Sun came up, just like a rose,
The one call'd *Heaven's eye*:
I'd plagiarize what you propose—
To butter up, and die.

So, peace be with you, as your dust
Is coursing through the waves
Of bygone eras, lent in trust
A golden spirit paves:

For where is heart, if not in art?
You trod the sod of time
Far from discreetly—to depart
Just in the nick of rhyme...

The poet powers waking hours
Onto beds of dung—
To grow wit's flowers, making towers
Wanting meadows, sung.

You laugh off Hell—does it exist?
At least, you say, for you
There is composed another list—
Admitted hitherto.

Rubber Band

Let Adam be imperial,
The sunlight and the view
So eloquent, ethereal—
For, naked in the dew,

We meet the Lord Primeval, one
Enchanting, via wit,
The beat restored I grieve, all done,
As, champing at the bit,

It's time we see unraveling,
Beginning at the end
She brews, as pieces traveling
So willingly descend

T' inspire higher fires, eke
Out Her maternal rest—
In shy disguise with Maya's, meek
As toucans, blessing jest...

Apollo, slow, I have to go,
For Daphne's on her way:
My foe's in woe from mistletoe—
And *that*'s the price you pay!

Broken Dreams

Got nothing more to resurrect,
Got sunshine on my mind;
Know what I am—at least, I check'd,
Before my heart went blind.

If I am Arthur's Lancelot,
As errant as a Knight
Inclined to pin and prance a lot,
Until he can alight

Godiva, do not mourn for me—
I sought, and then I found
Sophia better, borne to see
Her oceanic ground...

So, broken dreams of innocence,
Immortal spur be mine:
A man, so not a winner, gents,
If aught be serpentine.

Peter's Pluck

[eleven]

To see contagious hooker done—
Incarcerate his grace
So apt to drag on, as per sun,
This candlelight replace,

I scan the sky, to see the Moon
So gibbous—let it wane;
Pray tell, Maria—make it soon—
Was Peter's pluck in vain?

Now summer snow is winter sleet—
Devices turn to rust;
My bread is in a freezer, meet
For pabulum's disgust.

This morning's dew is not okay:
Since Adam was a youth,
He had a right to, come what may,
Take serpentry—to boot!

Carp

[twelve]

His match is offering to burn
Those scales at my feet:
I bask in gory Pawns, to spurn
The matter I repeat

So deeply, lovers must resign,
Before we topple down
Conditions worn, too aquiline,
Befitting Heaven's clown...

Too busy frying fish, God's bud,
Too busy flying free:
The Champ's assessing Howard's cud—
My potty frenemy

Whose sting is in his tail, love,
Outrageous cumquat ray:
Too bad if I regale doves—
Hot crossing Santa Fe.

Stranger to my Heart

To give up hope, to see the stopper
Clamming up a soul:
And then to catch her smile—proper
Fork in sync we stole...

She crystalizes wisdom's love,
She Queens, to rise again;
In her, perhaps, a little dove
Will grace the savage glen

To let us be, to love and live,
To never leave her heart:
The spring of summer she must give,
Lest winter's plot impart

More menace, and, if time commence
Aflame, to quench and quell,
Allowing beaux and belles don dense
Compassion—just as well.

Saint Joseph

[fourteen]

My friend in Heaven, bless my soul,
For eyes just cannot see
What folly follows Vinnie's toll—
Dismissal meant for me.

O Lord, my sweet creator, God
Of majesty and might—
Restore my faith, a heavy wad
Of paper, like a kite

In broken pieces, wings and woe
Together, just as you
Felt sunset's hoe must come and go—
Again, so hard to do.

But stranger to your heart is she,
A damsel to your dolt:
We pillory your pedigree—
That savage thunderbolt!

Songbird

[fifteen]

The little, lovely, Lenten lass,
Whom letters cannot claim,
Is given unto hope, in Mass
Illiterate, and lame.

Her beauty smiles at her trips
To offer up, apace,
Her sacred lime and orange pips—
For lemons, in disgrace,

Are fizzing as I come along:
The songbird, in my cage,
Would sing if I were right or wrong—
As tern may be my gauge...

Believe her—if she skip or sink—
Do I? I might as well;
My Kitty's on a skating rink
Of starlight, in a shell.

Rambling Rosie

[sixteen]

I listen, clear, to better hear
The pitter patter of my hopes
Eloping, far from check or cheer—
Orang-Utans on slipp'ry slopes

So not so happy, in your nest—
Yet what rejoicing, in my heart,
Sprang up, t' endear my flute and crest
To reach that busted, bleeding part

You break in two—my soul asunder,
Crowns and thorns between my teeth:
Enlightenmental star of wonder,
Rising from a tomb beneath...

Concession is but short rebuke,
Tomorrow's rhododendron shot:
Dear John's a mark too matt for Luke—
In love with leaven, hot-to-trot.

Lest God We Fear

[seventeen]

A thunderclap, a lightning stroke,
And gentle, in between,
The God of Love—if He awoke,
So zealous, quick, and green

To love your children: Give them gas
To catechize, in choir,
Heaven's daughter—late for Mass,
To see the fog respire...

No problem—let us settle Mars,
But wait, we're soaking in
Nod's repetitious lines we parse,
To let all Hell begin:

They love to call a cripple cursed,
As if, once born of clay,
The Son of God was Abel, nursed,
To shake his blues away

In cobwebs and machinery—
Too late to wax in hope,
Adapting to the scenery's
Contempt for Herod's dope.

Coverings of Clay

[eighteen]

Blood dons a smile I must doff—
If soot, if sand, if salt
Be steam for kinsfolk sleeping rough,
Forgiveness for a colt

Once telling tales: Make them true,
And still my heart should ache,
To see my embers black 'n' blue—
For Yuletide's token sheik

Sweats coverings of clay, to pray
For souls, whose sight is wont
To see Him canvass curds 'n' whey
Beneath the clouds I don't...

Yet I, perchance, so hippity—
Forgive me if I bruise—
Pluck sense and serendipity,
From riverbeds I choose

To settle on, as Abraham
Lets butter fly for three
Too nettlesome: Bedazzle Sam,
If *He* won't set you free!

Living's Given

[nineteen]

Tusk, tusk, they say, you'd better count
Your pennies, till they drop—
As butter splutters beds, a fount
For when these dills may stop:

For thee, my Jewess, do I pledge,
Upon your sloping lawns,
To elongate a lesser hedge
Of infidels, in thorns—

Loss leaders taking up the torch,
From failing hands bewept:
If jealous heads hot Hells debauch,
'Tis Eden's lover swept

Forevermore in new days, won
So wantonly, to chase
This warlock's black 'n' blue days—gone
So lost in your embrace

This lack of ethics, with the fruit
Of spirit: love, joy, peace,
Forbearance—never to dilute
That kindness you police

With goodness, faithfulness as well,
As gentleness of soul
No more awaits the Gates of Hell,
Applying self-control.

No Sewer

[twenty]

J'accuse! You love to plant your moss,
To let me dangle where
That rolling stone I come across
Will shatter, in mid air:

Evil woman, count me sewn,
Before I'm counting ghee
You're swishing in, each pallid bone
So not in love with me.

The Queen of Hearts? *The Nine of Spades*!
Far tins recapture what
Your memories made *Everglades*—
Creek Tribulation's knot...

A sewer am I? Why not slay
Your snakes on *Lover's Lawn*?
Just tell me I'm about to bay—
Bewail I was born.

Quietly Contrary

[twenty-one]

I know not for whom soul so quick
Elects to clamber, climb—
To navel-gaze, I am too thick,
Too lemon, to be lime.

Yes, I who caught what love aborts,
To snatch desire's train,
Would sell it all, too blind of sorts,
If fondly love remain.

Jehovah—ogre in my heart,
That *potpourri of loss*—
I sense my sandals worn, to chart
A bridge too far to cross—

Lest hope ensnare what, ripp'd in two,
My brethren lend a hand
To prepossess, in Kathmandu,
Snow sinking, quick as sand

So quietly contrary—gone
Am I, to bleed for her?
She's up to what Dick Whittington
Would fabulate, inter!

My Aim Is True

Atypical she is, you bet;
Magnificent, perhaps:
Am I a man, or must I let
Voluptuous her claps

Admonish me, so wittingly—
Her quintessential heart's
Ascent of cherries, pitting me
To ruin what departs?

May hope abound—I stand my ground,
Yet she is one to win—
Lest I impede another sound,
Soft immanence begin,

So still I cannot move this water
Lapping ocean's claw—
Till love, in loving, prove my daughter:
Gazing on her shore.

The Sun in Winter

[twenty-three]

She springs through winter, set in stone,
On decking left to stain;
If needs be, give her dog a bone,
Then let it off its chain.

We mystify our enemies—
In offerings of myrrh,
Gold, frankincense, intent to please,
Intrinsically cur

Upon a search for answers, not
One soul is apt to lose,
Until desire's Panzers plot
Their follies trapp'd, infuse

Inadequate temptations—that's
A virtue mine to cross:
Deceiver of the Nations, brat's
Ailurophobic moss.

The Art in Jazz

[twenty-four]

This morning, I am on the move—
This video I glean
Is writing on the wall, to prove
There's kids we haven't seen.

So wont am I to weep, as willows
Whispering in shrouds
Of tantalizing truth, a pillow's
Domicile, in clouds.

She's got a heart another held,
To free a captive bird;
To herald sun the darkness melds
With melodies unheard

To venture forth, courageous, not
To quibble, nor to shirk
What's teaming wit, to get her hot...
If all the World's a kirk!

Lover

[twenty-five]

The Sun is risen, Hope adorns
Szabóné she must be—
Ascamper over heathen lawns,
Bequeathing savagery.

Yet where is she, now lost to view,
Albeit clean of heart?
Star ever prudent, ever true,
From whom I should depart

Reluctantly, although I can
Remember ginger eyes:
Two searchlights on a better man
For being hers to prize...

A moment altogether lost,
For all my witness shows:
To drive all night, to pay the cost
Again—why, Heaven knows!

So Many Personalities

[twenty-six]

A beautiful delinquent, such
As I am wont to be,
She's even taking off his crutch—
For generosity

Of spirit-soul, this body's house,
She's putting on a plane:
A cat she is for this ole mouse—
Let sunshine pray for rain!

"Ridiculous!" she purrs—or neighs,
Jane Austen, tell me which—
Due connotations are a phase,
Parameters we pitch

To stigmatize the sensitive,
Mere orphans of her sweet
Liaisons: May her dense wit live
Between two kinds of treat.

Honeysuckle Hues

[twenty-seven]

How may I play, this day, for thee,
To sew a plover's lips?
I pocket gamma rays, to see
Fleet Huckleberry trips

Through history, a mystery
Our song in credit won—
Lest sunlight, sworn to sisterly
Seclusion, edit fun...

Still, I shall keep the best of me,
Now standing in a sphere's
Periphery—in quest of thee
Seceding to the jeers

With mental pabulum, my genes
Of denim, in despair,
To bless tomorrow's dawn: my Queen's
Elusive ruby hair...

For I can see a cock that crew
Three times, before, denied,
Lord Nelson's team, my Waterloo,
Grew up, to open wide

Our fire's inner bonny cot:
How choirs choose to muse
On her—to win her honey pot
In honeysuckle hues.

The Rose

[twenty-eight]

Five-point-eight millennia
Are gone, on tippy toes—
Their legacy's a Penny, *adieu*'s
Peace, infecting Rose...

The Truth can hurt: Am I, untrue,
A question to revive?
Reports we may dismiss undo
This lamington, alive

A humble bumblebee my Sam:
Our scenery's a hive
To buzz, together, free—why, Ma'am,
Let Queenery deprive

The soldier crab, the scorpion,
Tarantula we blame,
Of gen'ral merit, poor paeans
The Killer's will to tame

The Lion and the Lamb, the Lord
From Love's beginning woke—
'Tis Abel Adam must applaud:
The Son of Man's a bloke!

Middle Covenant

[twenty-nine]

So suddenly your God of Fear
Became the Prince of Peace—
That rod, O Solomon, revere
Like Saul, to find release.

I cannot fathom ev'ry drop
Of sunlight in the snow;
But speak to me of sadness, lop
That middle, wooden bow—

And, Prince of Glory, see Him there,
So pinion'd on His crutch—
Or rather two, like steak so rare,
For us to hurt as much

As all I am, division gone,
This morning being broke,
Albeit darkness, well and wan
Together, nearly spoke—

To twist and turn, eternities
Of never-ending loss:
Must I look up, to learn what He's
Conceding, on a cross?

Oh So Awesomely

[thirty]

O Dear, lest thou be hunted, tend
Thine art, as good as gold,
In escapades a lion, friend
To children, young and old,

To whom, in whispers of thy breast,
That gentle, loving room,
This night shall, in demand, so rest
Until the morrow's bloom...

The links thou, serendipitous,
May leave to light, in lore,
Match *Minne*'s tears, lent cinemas
In riveting *rapport*:

Two eyes thy love long lifted, veil
Unto meek and mild,
Be comeliness, at once the Grail
And the little child—

So, *Angelita*, guide my star,
To be what Faith prefers:
Of four a friend, my field far
From winning she that purrs.

In Flanders Square

[thirty-one]

In Flanders Square an obelisk
Will set in stone regret—
And so, we men, to run a risk,
Propitiate its net.

Yet hopes in hale hearts implant
Our faith in God, to win
The battle for the truth we chant—
The Evil One to bin

Lest children, borne to live on Earth,
Perceive what Men from Mars,
Or mercenaries given birth,
Would polish off, in scars...

Five wars—Korea, Vietnam,
Malaya in between—
Post which our meek and mild lamb,
To brave the smutty scene,

Best come again, in glory, wash
Cork wicks and woes away—
Lest mud and slime engulf galoshes'
Corners: Let us pray.

Lenco's Lass

He oughtn't to have left his love—
He did, and half of her
Left with him, to the Light above:
Gold, frankincense, or myrrh

In seventh Heaven, taking me
His grace to see and hear—
The greatest poet Love may be,
In searching for an ear.

His *Book of Longing*, this and more
So beautifully hers
To look, belonging, wishing for
What eloquence defers:

Maman, tu sais que je t'adore—
Pourquoi, c'est évident—
You know what *Esperanza*'s for:
Two lovers, knowing want,

Shall see you part your chestnut hair
In never-ending leaves—
A stallion waiting on a mare's
Blue majesty he weaves

As King and Queen of Love, immune
Art's prisoner, too fell
On wing—lest Genie's dove impugn
Heart risen, unto Hell.

Forevermore So White

[thirty-three]

Madonna, callow was your skin
Your Joseph kind forgot—
Othello's fellow in a spin,
Two weak for tommyrot

In quelling nights: I see a sac,
Patrolling, like a stone,
Tomorrow's bleak injustice, back
When Eva was a bone…

Here's hoping years of shifting sands,
So nettlesome and meek,
Won't settle like your dove that lands
On Zephaniah's peak:

For I shall make a pure tongue,
That all may comprehend
The Word of sweet Jehovah's lung—
Beginning at the end.

In searching for His sanction, I,
So verily in love
With love, impute redemption's guy—
Whose jealous, zealous glove

Doth, reaching out, beseech my heart,
To, weeping tears of hope,
Take up His cudgel, mini-mart
Beyond a spire's scope.

Woman's Irony

[thirty-four]

Now, iron these shirts,
You are mine to possess:
The sex kitten purrs—
If you'd let me undress,

To doff all my coverings,
Nearly before
The plover your heron sings
Wantonly for...

I'm veak—on the chessboard
And dire in bed:
I'd play you, across sward,
On fire instead

To see my calamities:
Write me a book
Impeding insanity's
Chalice and chook

To chant lines a lemon
Configures in time:
You can't beat a woman
Select and sublime

Here up on a high shelf—
A beauteous sea
In which doctors know myself
Better than me!

Dark Squares

[thirty-five]

Unbeatable foe—are you Jesus? For sure!
You must've been Hitler, a few years before;
Yes, better with practice, that rant on the hill
Abom'nable, murderous, manic, and ill,
Foreshadows the Holocaust—just to get back
At one judging justly: that whippet, jet black!

But wait, O despicable Son of a Gun,
Doth not Adonai pretend Adam's His Son?
For you, Son of Man, in a rush to be Cain,
Intuit the Killer, lest terror remain...

So, what if you're Abel, descry from the earth
A woman so vile about to give birth
To Seth, amongst others—a hard case to sell
If X marks the spot, whither both of you fell
To earth: Mere co-incidence? Probably, though
There isn't too much of it, *Belle* for a *Beau*...

'Tis clear to the rest of us, willing to learn
How dark is *the Jester*'s up-skilling: To burn,
Assemble eternity, one with the lot
For embers' fraternity, someone forgot.

Ship of Fools

For Friedrich Schiller, rich in peace,
God's listening—no room
For Mounties, gendarmes, or police
Too glistening, on Zoom...

My friend, you can't restore yourself
By ceding more respect,
For snowflakes, inner tortoise shell,
Forever poor reflect

On sonnets writ unwritable—
Your single-digit spree
For matadors unfightable,
Impossible as she

Can don the scone, O Son of Bonn,
To whom the cheery pack
Of legendary pirates on
The Ship of Fools we hack

Ineffably, in sweet revenge,
See cane-toads crawling loose
Beneath what's left of ole Stone Henge—
In sempiternal juice.

What?

[thirty-seven]

What, did I hear you put a word
To what I needn't say?
Our pussycats are often heard
To give the game away...

My spite's quite potent, and contempt
For cretins is immense:
Those homophobes, so cool, so kempt,
Epitomizing Lents

On Christmases, where all that rot—
Just ask Alicia Keys—
Will get you burning up like snot
That crackles into cheese...

Why should I chat to little boys?
Am I a Catholic priest?
I hear Bob Dylan over noise,
From which we are released:

"A medal pinn'd on Everest!"
Let Leonard Cohen deem
Another's clear endeavour best—
And teach him how to dream.

Tiffany

[thirty—eight]

Hey, Tiffany, a whiff of thee
Inclining me to sniff
Epiphanies, so niftily
Inspiring and stiff

This photograph, inside my brain,
Albeit fading fast,
Is starlight, inner choir's pain,
For, seeking love at last,

Tents come and go—the one we share,
Emporium of glue—
Bat, mitt far kitten's prickly pear,
Before it's bitten you!

Bojangles' dance, across the cell—
As brutal as it seems,
Just one of us will knock on Hell's
Dark portal Hope redeems.

As Clear as Calm at Sea

[thirty-nine]

O sweet Maria, dry my ducts,
And wrest my love from angst;
Trees, in the gentle breeze, a flux
In time may turn to planks

I for thee walk: Am I the Fiend,
God's pirate in the black—
Like Newton by the apple bean'd,
For trying whom I sac?

Still, I remember who you are;
I follow, in the rain,
The dusk and dawn of ev'ry scar
That ever caused you pain:

You're nursing me, new woman kind,
In answer to my quest,
To take what I in succour find—
And pronto, blest by test!

Adonai

forty

'Tis uncondition'd lust we trust—
For we have been deceived
By gusts five decades, pawning rust,
Will beggar, misconceived:

A further dust cannot efface
Our Bobby on the beat—
Let's gather on his interface
To lobby love *élite*,

His trail's pale modesty
To entertain the sting
In jail's tale—God bless thee,
Two lovebirds on each wing…

We'll sing a song King Solomon
Should never leave unsung—
Like rubies, precious, wild, a swan
Tectonic on your tongue.

Hashem, your turning, trembling globe
Is *manna* on a plate
For someone in a purple robe—
And James, so hard to mate.

"It is finish'd!"

www.ingramcontent.com/pod-product-compliance
Lightning Source LLC
Chambersburg PA
CBHW031238120626
46545CB00003B/1178